GOVERNING POLICIES OF NOMINEE DAKOTA FRANDSEN

Governing Policies of Nominee Dakota Frandsen

DAKOTA FRANDSEN

CONTENTS

#12　　73

INTRODUCTION

In pursuit of a strategic advisory role within key government agencies through the "Nominees for the People" initiative presented by Robert Kennedy Jr under the second administration of President Donald Trump, Dakota Frandsen brings an exceptional blend of entrepreneurial spirit, resilience, and a passionate advocacy for mental health, justice reform, and public integrity. With extensive expertise in empowering marginalized voices and a proven track record of inclusive leadership, Dakota is uniquely equipped to address the pressing and multifaceted issues facing national security, justice, and economic growth today. His platform, Bald and Bonkers Network LLC, not only demonstrates a steadfast commitment to accessible support systems but also fosters a culture of integrity, courage, and empathy across diverse communities that have often felt overlooked.

As a nominee for advisory positions across vital agencies such as the CIA, DHS, DOJ, USAGM, and SBA, Dakota's primary policies reflect an unwavering dedication to rebuilding trust and resilience within American institutions that have faced significant challenges. These policy pillars include enforcing term limits for elected officials to promote accountability, expanding mental health resources specifically for first responders who serve on the front lines, deprogramming harmful psychological influences that detrimentally affect individuals, and advocating for comprehensive victim support and rehabilitation accessibility for those struggling with addiction. His informed stance on misinformation, modern psychological operations, and public support for law enforcement reveals a profound commitment to addressing both visible and covert threats to public well-being, ensuring that security measures are inclusive and effective. Dakota's proposals resonate with the core principles of integrity, empathy, and inclusivity as he seeks to build an ecosystem where personal stories, entrepreneurial resources, and mental health support converge harmoniously for the betterment of society as a whole. Dakota's qualifications are evident through his honesty, integrity, and remarkable adaptability in both professional and personal realms.

Through Bald and Bonkers, he has cultivated a vibrant community where individuals can openly share experiences often considered unconventional or stigmatized. His unwavering transparency has empowered trauma survivors, individuals grappling with mental health challenges, and others to find a safe space for healing, proving his capacity to lead initiatives that are deeply rooted in empathy and truth. Dakota's impressive record and steadfast values position him as a candidate fully capable of fostering positive and transformative change within critical agencies, ensuring that the essence of public service is defined by courage, accountability, and a profound compassion for all members of society.

#1

Policy on Term Limits and Eligibility Requirements for Senators and Representatives

1. Purpose

The purpose of this policy is to establish term limits, ensure competency, and uphold ethical standards for Senators and Representatives within governing bodies. This policy aims to maintain integrity, accountability, and public trust in legislative functions.

2. Term Limits

- **Term Restriction**: No Senator or Representative shall serve more than **two consecutive terms** within any governing body, regardless of agency or branch.

- **Definition of a Term**: A term is defined as the complete duration of elected service as prescribed by law for Senators and Representatives within the relevant jurisdiction.

- **Non-Consecutive Service**: After serving two consecutive terms, an individual may not run for re-election until a full term has elapsed since the end of their last term in office.

3. Eligibility Requirements for Continued Service

- **Annual Competency Evaluations**:

  - All Senators and Representatives are required to undergo **annual physical and mental health evaluations** to ensure the continued competency necessary for their roles.
  - Evaluations must be conducted by independent and licensed medical professionals appointed by a designated ethics oversight committee.
  - Failure to pass these evaluations will result in immediate suspension from office, pending a thorough review.

- **Felony Investigation Restrictions**:

  - Any Senator or Representative who is the **subject of an active felony criminal investigation** is temporarily suspended from participating in legislative decision-making processes.
  - Investigations that involve potential abuse of power or attempts to influence legal proceedings must be disclosed to the ethics oversight committee.
  - Suspension remains in place until the investigation is resolved; if no charges are filed, full reinstatement is permitted.

4. Criminal Accountability and Sentencing for Abuse of Power

- **Standard for Conviction**: Senators or Representatives found guilty of felony crimes involving abuse of office must have been convicted with evidence meeting the threshold of **"beyond a reasonable doubt."**
- **Sentencing Enhancements**:

  - If found guilty of abusing their position of power to manipulate laws, statutes, or criminal processes for personal gain, the following additional penalties shall apply:

    - **Extended Sentencing**: An automatic **20-year enhancement** added to the criminal sentence.
    - **Capital Punishment Consideration**: For severe crimes meeting the legal requirements for capital punishment, the death penalty may be pursued, based on the crime's gravity and jurisdictional laws.
- **Ethics and Oversight Committee Role**: An independent ethics and oversight committee will review all cases of abuse of office, ensuring sentencing aligns with legal and ethical standards.

5. Policy Review and Amendments

- **Regular Review**: This policy shall be reviewed every **five years** by the ethics oversight committee to ensure compliance with evolving legal standards and public expectations.

- **Amendment Process**: Any amendments must be proposed by the ethics committee and approved through the legislative process to ensure transparency and adherence to democratic principles.

6. Implementation and Compliance

- **Responsibility for Enforcement**: The ethics oversight committee, in collaboration with relevant judicial and law enforcement agencies, is responsible for ensuring compliance with this policy.
- **Transparency and Public Reporting**: Annual reports on term limits, evaluations, and investigation statuses of Senators and Representatives shall be published, while maintaining confidentiality where legally mandated.

Policy on Creating a Thriving Entrepreneurial Ecosystem

1. Purpose

This policy is designed to foster a supportive environment for small businesses by offering tax incentives, shielding them from unfair competition, providing accessible learning opportunities, and establishing certification programs. The goal is to cultivate an ecosystem where small businesses can thrive, maintain integrity, and build consumer trust.

2. Tax Breaks for Small Businesses

- **Eligibility for Tax Breaks**: Small businesses with fewer than 100 employees are eligible for annual tax deductions designed to encourage growth and job creation.
- **Incentive Details**:
  - **Job Creation Incentive**: Small businesses demonstrating increased hiring or consistent employment levels year over year are eligible for additional tax credits.
  - **Community Impact**: Businesses actively contributing to community development, job creation, and fair employment practices may qualify for further tax benefits.
- **Application Process**: Eligible businesses must apply annually, submitting records of employment and wage practices to the Small Business Association (SBA) for review and verification.

3. Protection from Large Corporations

- **Anti-Competitive Protection**: Small businesses will receive legal protections from large corporations attempting to engage in predatory pricing, monopolistic tactics, or other anti-competitive practices.
- **Buyout Safeguards**: Limitations will be established to prevent unsolicited buyouts by large corporations unless small business owners voluntarily seek acquisition.

- **Monitoring and Reporting**: A Small Business Oversight Board will oversee claims of anti-competitive practices and enforce legal actions where appropriate to safeguard fair competition.
- **Local Business Coalitions**: Small businesses are encouraged to form coalitions that support resource-sharing, co-marketing, and networking opportunities, enhancing their resilience against larger competitors.

4. Entrepreneurial Education through Low-Cost E-Learning Programs

- **Program Accessibility**: The SBA will provide low-cost e-learning courses tailored for small business owners and entrepreneurs to foster healthy, sustainable business practices.
- **Course Content**:

    - **Financial Literacy and Tax Management**: Courses on effective budgeting, bookkeeping, tax compliance, and growth forecasting.
    - **Ethical and Fair Hiring Practices**: Training on hiring, fair wage policies, and fostering a positive workplace culture.
    - **Digital Skills and Online Presence**: Courses covering social media management, digital marketing, e-commerce, and website development.

- ◦ **Artificial Intelligence in Business**: Instruction on how to responsibly integrate AI in business operations, with a focus on transparency, ethics, and efficiency.
- **Certification for Course Completion**: Participants who successfully complete courses will receive certificates that can be displayed to customers and partners as evidence of their commitment to sound business practices.

5. Small Business Association (SBA) Recommendation Certification Program

- **Objective**: To highlight businesses that offer unique products or services beneficial to other businesses and industries.
- **Eligibility and Requirements**: Businesses must apply to the program, demonstrating innovation, quality, and ethical business practices.
- **Evaluation and Certification**: Selected businesses undergo a review process conducted by the SBA, focusing on the value of their offerings to the entrepreneurial community.
- **Certification Benefits**: Certified businesses are featured on the SBA's resource list for small businesses, which is accessible to the public as a trusted directory of recommended resources.

6. Small Business Association Certification Program for Influencers and Business Owners

- **Objective**: To provide a verifiable layer of trust for consumers and collaborators by certifying influencers, small business owners, and professionals.
- **Certification Process**:

  - **Application and Verification**: Interested individuals and businesses must submit an application with verifiable references, business records, and proof of ethical conduct.

  - **Evaluation Criteria**: Applicants are reviewed for integrity, legal compliance, transparency in business operations, and fair treatment of employees.

  - **Public Verification**: Certified individuals and businesses receive a unique SBA certification badge, which is listed in an SBA public registry and can be used in marketing and public relations.

7. Professional Conduct Review Board

- **Purpose and Composition**: The SBA will establish a Professional Conduct Review Board responsible for monitoring and upholding standards of behavior for certified small business owners and influencers.
- **Responsibilities of the Review Board**:

  - **Annual Review**: Conduct annual reviews of certified individuals and businesses to ensure compliance with ethical and legal standards.

- **Complaint Handling**: Investigate complaints from employees, consumers, or partners regarding violations of fair conduct, transparency, or legal compliance.
  - **Transparency and AI Integration**: Verify that certified businesses and individuals disclose any integration of Artificial Intelligence (AI) in their operations and ensure responsible use.
- **Standards for Certification Holders**:

  - **Legal Compliance**: Businesses must adhere to all legal requirements relevant to their industry.
  - **Fair Wage Practices**: Employees must be paid fair wages in line with local and industry standards.
  - **Professional Conduct**: Maintain a fair and respectful workplace, promoting a safe and positive culture between employees and management.
  - **AI Disclosure Requirements**: Businesses utilizing AI must provide clear information on how AI is used within their operations, ensuring transparency for customers and employees.
- **Consequences of Non-Compliance**:

  - **Warning and Probation**: For minor infractions, the board may issue a warning and place the business on probation for a specified period.

- ° **Certification Revocation**: Serious or repeated violations may result in revocation of SBA certification and disqualification from further SBA programs and resources.
- ° **Public Notice**: In cases of certification revocation, a public notice will be issued to maintain consumer trust.

8. Policy Review and Amendments

- **Annual Review**: This policy will be reviewed annually by the SBA to ensure relevance and effectiveness in meeting the needs of the small business ecosystem.
- **Amendment Process**: Amendments must be proposed by the SBA and approved by relevant government oversight bodies, with public input where appropriate, to maintain transparency and alignment with community needs.

#2

Policy on Therapy and Mental Health Support for First Responders, and Mental Health Programs in Professional and School Settings

1. Purpose

This policy establishes guidelines and advocacy efforts to enhance the mental health resources available to first responders, improve public perception and cooperation, and create educational programs aimed at fostering trust between first responders and the community. It also seeks to reform the criminal justice system by identifying root causes of crime and implementing educational resources to deter criminal behavior.

2. Mental Health Funding and Support for First Responders

- **Advocacy for Funding**: The policy advocates for dedicated mental health funding for first responder agencies at the state, county, and local levels. This funding is essential to:

    - Ensure that employees have access to confidential mental health services.

○ Provide support tailored to the unique challenges faced by first responders, such as trauma counseling and resilience training.

○ Establish wellness programs that allow first responders to access ongoing support for maintaining mental well-being throughout their careers.

- **Confidential Access to Resources**: Agencies should implement systems that allow first responders to seek mental health support confidentially, without fear of stigma or career repercussions. This includes:

    ○ Creating dedicated, off-site facilities where responders can access services outside of their workplace.

    ○ Enabling secure digital platforms for virtual counseling and resources, accessible around the clock.

- **Periodic Mental Health Check-ins**: Agencies should institute mandatory, confidential mental health evaluations at regular intervals to promote early intervention and provide support as needed.

3. Improving the Public Image of First Responders and Promoting Public Cooperation

- **Public Awareness Campaigns**: Launch campaigns that:

- ○ Highlight the dedication and sacrifices of first responders to their communities.
  - ○ Emphasize the critical role they play in maintaining public safety and community well-being.
- **Encouraging Timely Crime Reporting**: Educate the public on the importance of timely reporting of criminal activity and the value of cooperating with law enforcement for the safety of the entire community.
- **Community Outreach Programs**: Facilitate on-going community engagement programs where first responders can interact with the public, answering questions and providing resources to foster trust and cooperation.

4. Training First Responders to Recognize Signs of Mental Duress and Burnout in Colleagues

- **Mental Health Awareness Training**: All first responders will receive training to recognize signs of mental duress, stress, and burnout in their colleagues, including:

  - ○ Training on identifying symptoms of mental fatigue, PTSD, and burnout.
  - ○ Guidance on how to approach colleagues showing signs of mental distress, with an emphasis on peer support.

- **Peer Support Programs**: Establish peer support groups within agencies where first responders can share experiences and seek guidance in a non-judgmental environment.
- **Chain of Support Referrals**: Implement a system where first responders can refer colleagues for mental health resources confidentially, promoting early intervention and supporting mental wellness within the team.

5. School and Community Programs for Youth Engagement with First Responders

- **Youth Awareness Programs**: Schools should include programs that introduce children to the roles of first responders, fostering respect and trust in law enforcement, firefighting, and emergency medical services.
- **Interactive Safety Education**: Schools and youth centers can host interactive presentations with first responders, including:

    ◦ Demonstrations of safety protocols and the responsibilities of first responders.
    ◦ Programs that allow children to interact with first responders in a positive setting, building trust and understanding.
- **Inclusion of Diversity and Respect**: Programs will be inclusive, ensuring children from all back-

grounds understand that first responders are accessible, safe, and trustworthy resources in times of need.

6. Systemic Review and Rehabilitation of Incarcerated Citizens

- **Pattern Identification and Review**: A system will be implemented to analyze the circumstances of incarcerated citizens and identify patterns that contribute to criminal behavior, including socioeconomic challenges, education gaps, and lack of access to resources.
- **Policy Amendments for Crime Prevention**: Based on findings, policy amendments may be proposed to address root causes, focusing on crime prevention strategies such as:

    - Expanding educational resources in communities to reduce the appeal of criminal actions.
    - Allocating appropriate resources for mental health and addiction recovery programs.

- **Rehabilitation and Resource Division**: Resources will be divided to support rehabilitative programs, aiming to prepare convicted individuals for reintegration into society. Programs include:

    - Vocational training, educational programs, and mental health support for inmates.

- Support systems post-incarceration, focusing on reducing recidivism by offering stable resources and career pathways.
- **Transparency and Community Engagement**: Results of the systemic review will be shared with relevant community groups and stakeholders to ensure accountability and gain feedback for continuous improvement.

7. Professional Standards and Accountability

- **Mental Health Standards for All First Responders**: This policy affirms a commitment to maintaining high mental health standards across all first responder agencies.
- **Confidential Reporting Channels**: A confidential reporting system will be available to first responders to report any mental health or misconduct concerns within their departments.
- **Public Oversight and Input**: The community will be invited to participate in feedback sessions, ensuring that the measures taken meet the needs and expectations of the public.

#3

Policy on Rehabilitation Accessibility for Individuals with Substance Use Disorders

1. Purpose

This policy is designed to create accessible and effective pathways to rehabilitation for individuals with substance use disorders, particularly those arrested for drug possession or trafficking. By focusing on treatment, education, and supportive career opportunities, the policy aims to reduce recidivism, address root causes of addiction, and foster lasting recovery.

2. Rehabilitation as an Alternative to Sentencing for Individuals Charged with Drug Possession (with Intent to Use)

- **Eligibility for Reduced Sentencing**: Individuals arrested and charged with drug possession (with intent to use) are eligible for a reduced sentence if they choose to enter a state-approved drug rehabilitation program. This approach prioritizes addressing the underlying causes of addiction, helping individuals to:

- Engage in a structured rehabilitation program that addresses both physical and psychological aspects of substance dependence.
- Work with certified addiction specialists to explore factors contributing to substance use, such as mental health issues, trauma, or socio-economic challenges.

- **Program Requirements**: Eligible individuals must complete a designated duration and level of treatment, as determined by a licensed addiction specialist, in order to qualify for a reduction in their sentence.

- **Post-Rehabilitation Support**: Upon completion of the rehabilitation program, participants will have access to ongoing support resources, including counseling, job training, and placement programs, to support their reintegration into society.

3. Reduced Sentencing for Individuals Charged with Drug Trafficking Who Cooperate with Law Enforcement

- **Incentives for Cooperation**: Individuals arrested and charged with drug trafficking are eligible for a reduced sentence if they:

  - Cooperate fully with law enforcement agencies to provide accurate and actionable information on the structure and operations of criminal drug networks.

- ◦ Assist in identifying key figures, methods of trafficking, and other critical information that can aid in dismantling criminal organizations.

- **Protective Measures**: In order to protect cooperating individuals and ensure they are not targeted by drug networks, law enforcement agencies will provide necessary protective measures for participants, including, if needed, witness protection.

- **Evaluation of Cooperation**: The reduction in sentencing will be determined based on the value and completeness of the information provided, as assessed by a designated law enforcement official or committee.

4. Formation of an Addiction and Rehabilitation Advisory Board

- **Composition of the Advisory Board**: An expert advisory board will be established, composed of top-ranking psychologists, addiction specialists, social workers, and medical professionals.

- **Responsibilities**: The advisory board will be responsible for:

  - ◦ Observing and documenting trends in addiction, new drug types, and usage patterns, providing a data-backed perspective on emerging public health challenges.
  - ◦ Defining necessary qualifications and classifications of addiction severity to create a stan-

dardized approach to identifying and treating addiction.

- ◦ Offering evidence-based recommendations for treatment protocols, prevention programs, and policy updates to representatives and relevant government bodies.
- **Ongoing Research and Prevention Measures**: The board will also support government agencies in creating preventive education campaigns to raise awareness and mitigate substance abuse trends, ensuring that policies remain responsive to new developments in addiction research.

5. Medical and Vocational Training Programs to Support Rehabilitation and Career Development

- **Medical Training Opportunities**: Individuals in rehabilitation programs will have access to training and certification in medical and health-related fields, which provide a fulfilling career path post-rehabilitation. This initiative serves to:

    - ◦ Encourage participants to maintain sobriety and provide them with the skills to succeed in a career that gives back to their communities.
    - ◦ Offer a unique pathway for former addicts to contribute positively to healthcare, addiction treatment, and peer support services.
- **Vocational Skills Development**: In addition to medical training, individuals may choose from a va-

riety of vocational training programs that align with their interests and strengths. Examples include certification programs in technology, construction, social services, and counseling.

- **Job Placement Assistance**: Post-rehabilitation, program participants will be supported by job placement services that connect them with employers willing to hire individuals in recovery, helping to ensure a smooth transition back into the workforce and providing a stable foundation for a successful and sober life.

6. Evaluation and Accountability

- **Outcome Tracking**: All participants in the rehabilitation programs will be tracked through an evaluation system that assesses long-term outcomes, including rates of relapse, employment stability, and recidivism. Data gathered will inform future policy improvements and program adjustments.
- **Regular Policy Review**: This policy will be reviewed annually by the advisory board and relevant stakeholders to incorporate feedback, track progress, and address emerging challenges in addiction and rehabilitation.
- **Transparency and Public Reporting**: Summaries of program success rates and improvements will be published periodically to keep the public informed about the effectiveness and societal impact of these rehabilitation initiatives.

4

Policy on the Criminalization and Regulation of Tobacco Products

1. Purpose

This policy aims to eliminate the production, sale, and use of tobacco products by 2030, recognizing the adverse health and social impacts associated with tobacco. Through increased taxes, penalties, and support services, this policy seeks to reduce tobacco dependency, allocate funds toward education, and explore beneficial alternatives such as medicinal marijuana and industrial hemp.

2. Increased Taxes on Tobacco Sales and Businesses

- **Taxation on Tobacco Products**: Effective immediately, a substantial increase in taxes will be imposed on the sale of all tobacco products. This includes a rise in excise taxes on individual product sales as well as licensing fees for businesses selling tobacco products.

- **Business Licensing Fees**: Any new or existing business seeking to sell tobacco products must pay significantly higher licensing fees. These fees will act as a disincentive while helping to fund public initiatives related to education, research, and law enforcement.

- **Allocation of Funds**: Revenue generated from increased taxes and fees will be allocated as follows:

  - **Education Funding**: A portion of the revenue will be invested in public education initiatives aimed at preventing youth tobacco use and raising awareness about the dangers of tobacco.
  - **Law Enforcement**: Funds will support law enforcement efforts related to the regulation and gradual elimination of tobacco products.
  - **Research into Marijuana and Hemp**: Resources will be allocated to research into the potential medicinal benefits of marijuana and industrial uses for hemp as viable alternatives to tobacco, contributing to a shift toward safer, legal alternatives.

3. Total Criminalization of Tobacco by 2030

- **Gradual Phase-Out and Final Criminalization**: A step-by-step approach will be implemented to phase out all aspects of tobacco production, sales, and manufacturing, culminating in the complete criminalization of tobacco by 2030. This will involve:

  - **Manufacturing Restrictions**: All tobacco manufacturing will be regulated strictly, with progressive restrictions on production capacity until the 2030 deadline.

- ○ **Sales and Distribution Limitations**: Licensed retailers will face increasingly restrictive sales quotas, gradually reducing the availability of tobacco products until a complete sales ban is in place.
- ○ **Criminal Penalties Post-2030**: After 2030, any individual or business involved in the production, sale, or distribution of tobacco products will be subject to criminal penalties; including fines, loss of business licensing, and potential imprisonment.

4. Support Services and Cost Reductions for Tobacco Cessation

- **Subsidized Quit-Programs**: Tobacco users seeking to quit will have access to subsidized cessation programs, including counseling, therapy, nicotine replacement therapies, and approved medications at reduced costs.
- **Public Health Initiatives**: Additional funding will be allocated to public health campaigns that promote a smoke-free lifestyle and encourage tobacco users to pursue cessation options.
- **Employer Incentives for Quit Programs**: Employers will be incentivized to offer workplace-based cessation programs, including paid time for participa-

tion in quit programs and access to tobacco cessation
resources.

5. Enforcement of Penalties for Minors with Tobacco Products

- **Parental Responsibility and Fines**: Heavy fines
  will be imposed on parents or legal guardians of minors found in possession of tobacco products, recognizing the critical role of parental supervision in
  preventing youth tobacco use.
- **Educational and Corrective Actions**: In addition to financial penalties, parents and minors may be
  required to attend educational sessions on the risks of
  tobacco use and the legal implications of underage tobacco possession.
- **School and Community Reporting Systems**:
  Schools and community programs will be empowered
  to report tobacco possession by minors to local law
  enforcement, triggering fines and corrective actions
  for parents while emphasizing community engagement in tobacco prevention.

6. Evaluation and Reporting

- **Annual Progress Reports**: The effectiveness of
  this policy will be assessed annually through progress
  reports that examine tax revenue, reduction in tobacco sales, participation in cessation programs, and
  legal enforcement statistics.

- **Transparency and Public Access to Information**: These reports will be made publicly available, ensuring transparency and public awareness of the progress toward tobacco elimination and the impact on public health and community welfare.

- **Continuous Adjustment**: The policy will be reviewed annually by a designated task force, with adjustments made as necessary to respond to emerging public health needs, trends in tobacco use, and advancements in addiction treatment.

5

Policy on the Prevention of Falsified Criminal Offenses and False Imprisonment of Innocent Individuals

1. Purpose

This policy establishes strict measures to deter and penalize individuals who knowingly make false criminal accusations with malicious intent, and holds accountable any judicial or law enforcement officers who may contribute to wrongful convictions. It aims to protect the integrity of the justice system and safeguard innocent individuals from false imprisonment.

2. Penalties for Knowingly Falsifying Criminal Accusations

- **Malicious Intent in False Accusations:**

    ◦ Any individual found to have knowingly and intentionally falsified criminal accusations with malicious intent will face criminal charges. Upon a determination of guilt:

- The individual shall be sentenced to a maximum of **ten years in prison**.
- A maximum fine will be imposed, set at **$15,000 or 20% of the individual's annual income**, whichever amount is greater.

- **False Accusations of a Sexual Nature:**

  - If the false accusations pertain to sexual misconduct, additional penalties will apply:

    - The individual who made the false accusations shall be **registered as a sex offender**.
    - If the false accuser is under the age of 18, they shall be **tried as an adult** under this policy.
    - Should it be found that a minor was coerced by parents or legal guardians to make the false accusations, those guardians will instead be **registered as sex offenders** and face the associated penalties.

3. Penalties for False Accusations Leading to Imprisonment

- **False Accusations Resulting in Wrongful Imprisonment:**

- If false accusations result in the wrongful imprisonment of an innocent individual, the accuser shall be penalized in proportion to the harm inflicted:

    - **Prison Sentence**: The accuser shall serve a sentence equivalent to the total time served by the falsely accused.
    - **Financial Penalty**: In addition to imprisonment, the accuser shall pay a fine of up to **$20,000 or 25% of their annual income**, whichever amount is greater.

- **False Accusations Leading to Death Penalty Sentencing:**

    - Should false accusations result in a sentence of **capital punishment** for the accused, the accuser shall be considered for the death penalty as a potential penalty.
    - In cases where an innocent person has been **executed due to false accusations**, the individual who made the false accusations shall instead receive a sentence of **life imprisonment without the possibility of parole.**

4. Accountability Measures for Judicial and Law Enforcement Misconduct

- **Tampering, Bias, or Misconduct by Judicial or Law Enforcement Officials:**

    - Should an investigation reveal that the judge presiding over the wrongful case or any member of law enforcement willingly engaged in misconduct, including but not limited to tampering with evidence, altering case details, intimidation, blackmail, or displaying bias or prejudice against any protected demographic, the following measures will be applied:

        - **Immediate Unpaid Suspension**: All officials involved will be placed on unpaid suspension during a comprehensive investigation.
        - **Rigorous Evaluation**: Each implicated individual will undergo a thorough evaluation to assess any potential misconduct or violations of legal and ethical standards.
        - **Penalties upon Conviction**:

            - **Imprisonment**: Upon conviction, each guilty party will face a maximum sentence of **25 years in prison**.

- **Revocation of Legal and Employment Rights**: All rights to practice law, hold any office in law enforcement, or engage in any legal position will be permanently revoked. Any benefits or pensions related to their roles will also be forfeited.
- **Capital Punishment**: If it is determined that the intentional misconduct was egregious, resulting in significant harm to the innocent individual or causing additional social harm, parties involved may be subject to the **death penalty**, contingent on the circumstances and severity of the case.

5. Implementation and Review

- **Oversight and Reporting**: A designated oversight committee shall review each case of proven false accusation or wrongful imprisonment and compile an annual report detailing findings, accountability measures, and recommendations to further protect innocent individuals.
- **Transparency and Public Access to Information**: This committee will make relevant information

accessible to the public to ensure transparency and build trust in the judicial process.

- **Continuous Policy Evaluation**: This policy shall undergo periodic review and updates to align with evolving legal standards, ensuring comprehensive protection against falsified offenses and unjust imprisonments.

6

Policy on Enhanced Protections for Victims of Domestic Violence and Child Abuse

1. Purpose

This policy is designed to improve protections for victims of domestic violence and child abuse, implement preventive measures, enforce strict penalties for offenders, and reform systems related to child welfare. The goal is to establish a framework that holds perpetrators accountable, protects vulnerable individuals, and addresses the root causes and long-term impacts of abuse.

2. Advisory Board of Psychologists and Social Work Experts

- **Establishment of a Multidisciplinary Board**:

    ◦ A board comprising leading psychologists, social workers, and legal experts will be established as advisors to government representatives. The board will focus on studying and providing guidance on issues related to domestic violence, child abuse, and family dynamics.

- **Research and Analysis Areas**:

  - **Psychological Reasons for Staying in Abusive Relationships**: Identifying underlying factors such as dependency, fear, trauma bonding, or lack of resources that may influence victims to remain in abusive situations.
  - **Parental Neglect and Favoritism**: Assessing why some parents may neglect children from previous relationships in favor of children with new partners, and determining possible interventions.
  - **Appeasement of Abusive Partners**: Exploring why some individuals allow their children to be endangered by abusive partners, including the impact of manipulation, threats, and psychological coercion.
  - **Sibling and Parental Abuse**: Identifying risk factors leading to sibling abuse, as well as cases where children abuse parents or legal guardians.
  - **Long-Term Psychological Effects of Abuse**: Documenting and analyzing the lasting impact of domestic violence and child abuse on victims' mental health, relationships, and future behavior.
  - **Foster and Adoption System Reform**: Proposing reforms to better protect children in

the foster and adoption systems, reduce placement disruptions, and ensure that children find
safe and supportive homes.

3. Penalties for Child Abuse and Domestic Violence Offenders

- **Stricter Sentencing for Parents and Legal Guardians:**

  - Offenders found guilty of abusing their chil-
    dren may face one or more of the following
    penalties based on the severity of the abuse:

    - **Fixed Prison Sentence**: A minimum
      of 30 years in prison for severe abuse
      cases.
    - **Financial Penalty**: A fine set at
      $10,000 or 5% of the offender's annual
      income, whichever is greater.
    - **Court-Mandated Therapy**: Offend-
      ers must undergo long-term, intensive
      therapy focused on addressing abusive
      tendencies and understanding the impact
      of their actions.
    - **Chemical Castration**: In severe sex-
      ual abuse cases, chemical castration may
      be ordered to prevent future harm.
    - **Violent Offender Registration**: Of-
      fenders will be registered as violent of-

fenders, ensuring public awareness of their status.

- **Death Penalty Consideration**: In the most extreme and aggravated cases, such as those involving prolonged torture, intentional severe harm, or cases where multiple children were victims, capital punishment may be considered.

4. Penalties for Failure to Report Abuse

- **Consequences for Family Members Who Fail to Report Abuse**:

  ○ If it is determined during an investigation that a family member was aware of ongoing abuse but did not report it to authorities, the following penalties will apply:

    - **Prison Sentence**: A fixed sentence of 5 years, or if the victim was under 18, 10 years. For victims under the age of 13, a 25-year sentence applies, with an additional 5 years per child affected.
    - **Financial Penalty**: A fine of up to $10,000 or 15% of the offender's annual income (whichever is less). In cases involving children under 18, the fine will be the latest estimated cost of raising a

child to 18 in the U.S. or 20% of the offender's income (whichever is greater).

- **Child Removal**: If the offender has other children in their custody, the children will be removed and placed with a suitable caregiver, preferably a family member with whom they have a healthy, preexisting relationship.

5. Reform of Social Services and Child Protective Services (CPS)

- **Enhanced Investigation Protocols for High-Risk Residences**:

  - If three or more reports of suspected abuse or neglect are filed for a single residence, CPS and local social services shall be authorized to conduct unannounced welfare checks at any time, to prevent abusers from hiding evidence of abuse.

  - If four or more reports of suspected abuse or neglect are filed for a single residence are unfounded, CPS and local social services shall be permitted to work in collaboration with necessary law enforcement agencies to pursue criminal charges in accordance with "Policy on the Prevention of Falsified Criminal Offenses and False Imprisonment of Innocent Individuals" as stated in section #5

- **Annual Refresher Training**:

  - All social workers and CPS agents will be required to complete annual "refresher" courses on current abuse trends, detection techniques, and the latest policies to address new types of abuse, ensuring that they remain vigilant and well-informed.

6. Prevention and Treatment Programs for Sexual Predators

- **Comprehensive Study of Sexual Predators**:

  - A dedicated research initiative will focus on identifying behaviors, risk factors, and other indicators associated with child predators to develop preventive strategies and reduce the occurrence of sexual abuse.
- **Action Plans to Break Cycles of Abuse**:

  - Based on the study's findings, action plans will be developed to prevent repetitive cycles of abuse, increase community awareness, and support victims in their recovery to minimize long-term psychological harm.

7. Implementation and Oversight

- **Oversight Committee**:

- An independent oversight committee will monitor the effectiveness of this policy, including the board of psychologists' findings, case outcomes for abusers, and CPS reform initiatives.

- **Public Reporting and Accountability**:

  - This committee will provide annual reports to the public and government bodies on policy outcomes, case studies, and areas for improvement in victim protection and offender accountability.

- **Continuous Evaluation and Policy Updates**:

  - This policy will undergo regular evaluations and updates as new research and data become available, ensuring that all measures remain effective in protecting victims and addressing abuse at all levels.

#7

Policy Proposal on Enhanced Protections for Victims of Domestic Violence and Child Abuse

1. Purpose

This policy is designed to improve protections for victims of domestic violence and child abuse, implement preventive measures, enforce strict penalties for offenders, and reform systems related to child welfare. The goal is to establish a framework that holds perpetrators accountable, protects vulnerable individuals, and addresses the root causes and long-term impacts of abuse.

2. Advisory Board of Psychologists and Social Work Experts

- **Establishment of a Multidisciplinary Board:**

    ◦ A board comprising leading psychologists, social workers, and legal experts will be established as advisors to government representatives. The board will focus on studying and providing guidance on issues related to domestic violence, child abuse, and family dynamics.

- **Research and Analysis Areas**:

  - **Psychological Reasons for Staying in Abusive Relationships**: Identifying underlying factors such as dependency, fear, trauma bonding, or lack of resources that may influence victims to remain in abusive situations.
  - **Parental Neglect and Favoritism**: Assessing why some parents may neglect children from previous relationships in favor of children with new partners, and determining possible interventions.
  - **Appeasement of Abusive Partners**: Exploring why some individuals allow their children to be endangered by abusive partners, including the impact of manipulation, threats, and psychological coercion.
  - **Sibling and Parental Abuse**: Identifying risk factors leading to sibling abuse, as well as cases where children abuse parents or legal guardians.
  - **Long-Term Psychological Effects of Abuse**: Documenting and analyzing the lasting impact of domestic violence and child abuse on victims' mental health, relationships, and future behavior.
  - **Foster and Adoption System Reform**: Proposing reforms to better protect children in

the foster and adoption systems, reduce placement disruptions, and ensure that children find safe and supportive homes.

3. Penalties for Child Abuse and Domestic Violence Offenders

- **Stricter Sentencing for Parents and Legal Guardians**:

  ○ Offenders found guilty of abusing their children may face one or more of the following penalties based on the severity of the abuse:

    - **Fixed Prison Sentence**: A minimum of 30 years in prison for severe abuse cases.
    - **Financial Penalty**: A fine set at $10,000 or 5% of the offender's annual income, whichever is greater.
    - **Court-Mandated Therapy**: Offenders must undergo long-term, intensive therapy focused on addressing abusive tendencies and understanding the impact of their actions.
    - **Chemical Castration**: In severe sexual abuse cases, chemical castration may be ordered to prevent future harm.
    - **Violent Offender Registration**: Offenders will be registered as violent of-

fenders, ensuring public awareness of their status.

- **Death Penalty Consideration**: In the most extreme and aggravated cases, such as those involving prolonged torture, intentional severe harm, or cases where multiple children were victims, capital punishment may be considered.

4. Penalties for Failure to Report Abuse

- **Consequences for Family Members Who Fail to Report Abuse:**

  - If it is determined during an investigation that a family member was aware of ongoing abuse but did not report it to authorities, the following penalties will apply:

    - **Prison Sentence**: A fixed sentence of 5 years, or if the victim was under 18, 10 years. For victims under the age of 13, a 25-year sentence applies, with an additional 5 years per child affected.
    - **Financial Penalty**: A fine of up to $10,000 or 15% of the offender's annual income (whichever is less). In cases involving children under 18, the fine will be the latest estimated cost of raising a

child to 18 in the U.S. or 20% of the offender's income (whichever is greater).

- **Child Removal**: If the offender has other children in their custody, the children will be removed and placed with a suitable caregiver, preferably a family member with whom they have a healthy, preexisting relationship.

5. Reform of Social Services and Child Protective Services (CPS)

- **Enhanced Investigation Protocols for High-Risk Residences**:
  - If three or more reports of suspected abuse or neglect are filed for a single residence, CPS and local social services shall be authorized to conduct unannounced welfare checks at any time, to prevent abusers from hiding evidence of abuse. Local law enforcement may be contacted for support in potential high-risk cases.
  - If a minimum of five reports of suspected abuse or neglect are filed for a single residence, and no such signs of either were found, CPS and local social services may work with necessary law enforcement agencies to penalize the reporting party for abuse of resources in accordance with policy **#6 Policy on the Prevention of Falsified Criminal Offenses and**

False Imprisonment of Innocent Individuals

- **Annual Refresher Training**:

    ○ All social workers and CPS agents will be required to complete annual "refresher" courses on current abuse trends, detection techniques, and the latest policies to address new types of abuse, ensuring that they remain vigilant and well-informed.

6. Prevention and Treatment Programs for Sexual Predators

- **Comprehensive Study of Sexual Predators**:

    ○ A dedicated research initiative will focus on identifying behaviors, risk factors, and other indicators associated with child predators to develop preventive strategies and reduce the occurrence of sexual abuse.

- **Action Plans to Break Cycles of Abuse**:

    ○ Based on the study's findings, action plans will be developed to prevent repetitive cycles of abuse, increase community awareness, and support victims in their recovery to minimize long-term psychological harm.

7. Implementation and Oversight

- **Oversight Committee:**

  - An independent oversight committee will monitor the effectiveness of this policy, including the board of psychologists' findings, case outcomes for abusers, and CPS reform initiatives.

- **Public Reporting and Accountability:**

  - This committee will provide annual reports to the public and government bodies on policy outcomes, case studies, and areas for improvement in victim protection and offender accountability.

- **Continuous Evaluation and Policy Updates:**

  - This policy will undergo regular evaluations and updates as new research and data become available, ensuring that all measures remain effective in protecting victims and addressing abuse at all levels.

8

Policy Proposal: Accessibility and De-Stigmatization of Mental Health Resources

Objective:

To make mental health resources accessible, effective, and culturally accepted while promoting public understanding and reducing stigma surrounding mental health challenges.

1. Advisory Board Formation

- Establish an **Advisory Board for Mental Health Accessibility and Innovation**, composed of experts from diverse subfields of psychology, psychiatry, neuroscience, and alternative mental health approaches.

- Responsibilities include:

  - Identifying barriers to accessing mental health care.
  - Advising on public awareness campaigns and policy amendments.
  - Evaluating the efficacy of alternative mental health interventions.
  - Developing action plans for nationwide implementation of accessible care.

2. Public Awareness Campaigns

- Launch a nationwide initiative to **destigmatize mental health support**, emphasizing the importance of seeking help.
- Key strategies:

  - Partner with celebrities and influencers who have publicly shared their mental health journeys to create relatable content.
  - Produce and disseminate educational materials, social media campaigns, and documentaries highlighting the benefits of mental health care and stories of recovery.
  - Integrate mental health education into school curriculums to normalize discussions on mental well-being.

3. Incentives for Employers

- Advocate for **tax breaks and financial incentives** for employers who:

  - Offer comprehensive mental health resources, including therapy, counseling, and stress management programs.
  - Implement Employee Assistance Programs (EAPs) with a focus on mental health.
  - Create workplace environments that support open conversations about mental health.

4. Work-Life Balance for Public Service Employees

- Mandate reforms to improve the **work-life balance** of public service employees, particularly emergency service personnel.
- Proposals include:

  - Mandatory mental health leave policies.
  - Flexible working hours to reduce burnout.
  - Access to specialized mental health programs tailored to the unique challenges faced by first responders and public servants.

5. Alternative Care Coverage

- Expand government-provided health care to include **alternative mental health treatments** proven effective through thorough scientific testing.
- Examples of alternative care methods:

  - Cognitive-behavioral therapy (CBT) and mindfulness-based interventions.
  - Art and music therapy.
  - Non-traditional therapies, such as animal-assisted therapy and eco-therapy.

6. Research and Development

- Allocate funding for research into **holistic and drug-free mental health methods**, emphasizing non-invasive, sustainable approaches to improving mental health.

- Encourage collaboration with universities, non-profits, and private institutions to:

  ○ Explore the efficacy of diet, exercise, and sleep management on mental health.
  ○ Study emerging techniques like virtual reality therapy and neurofeedback.
  ○ Promote community-based interventions to foster social connections and reduce isolation.

Expected Outcomes:

- Broader accessibility to mental health care across all demographics.
- Reduced stigma surrounding mental health issues and seeking care.
- Improved employee productivity and satisfaction due to workplace mental health initiatives.
- Enhanced quality of life for public service employees.
- A healthier, more resilient population through diverse care methods.

9

Policy Proposal: Prevention of Misinformation in Health Decisions

Objective:

To safeguard public health by ensuring accurate dissemination of health information, promoting transparency in health-related decisions, and holding accountable those who spread misinformation that leads to adverse health outcomes.

1. Investigation of Health-Related Claims

- Establish a **Health Misinformation Review Unit (HMRU)** responsible for:
    - Investigating claims that impact public health and safety.
    - Collaborating with scientific institutions, medical experts, and government agencies to verify the accuracy of public statements, products, and policies.
    - Releasing findings in publicly accessible reports to maintain trust and accountability.

2. Criminal Prosecution for Harmful Misinformation

- Enforce **criminal penalties** for individuals or entities found guilty of knowingly spreading health-related misinformation that results in significant public harm or adverse health effects.
- Penalties may include:
    - Fines proportional to the scale of harm caused.
    - Incarceration for deliberate or malicious disinformation campaigns.
    - Mandatory retraction and public correction of the false information.

3. Right to Defend Claims

- Permit those accused of spreading potential misinformation to **plead their case** by:
    - Presenting evidence supporting their claims.
    - Undergoing a rigorous peer review process by independent experts to determine the validity of their assertions.
    - Submitting findings to relevant agencies for further analysis and potential incorporation into public health policies if proven valid.

4. Transparency in Public Health Products

- Mandate **full transparency** in the development, approval, and distribution of health-related products, including:
    - Medicines, vaccines, supplements, and medical devices.
    - Products related to dietary restrictions, sanitation, and general health.

- Transparency requirements include:
  - Clear labeling of ingredients and potential side effects.
  - Publication of clinical trial data and safety assessments.
  - Open communication about manufacturing processes and quality controls.

5. International Cooperation for Consumer Safety

- Collaborate with international partners to:
  - **Pressure corporations** to adopt safe and healthy practices that prioritize consumer health.
  - Share data and best practices for combating misinformation and promoting transparency.
  - Create unified standards for product safety and public health measures.

6. Establishment of an Oversight Committee

- Create an **Independent Health Oversight Committee** with the following responsibilities:
  - Monitoring compliance with policies and procedures that prioritize evidence-based science.
  - Preventing the influence of personal biases or conflicts of interest in health-related decisions.
  - Advising on updates to regulations to reflect the latest scientific discoveries and health trends.

Expected Outcomes:

- A well-informed public capable of making health decisions based on accurate and transparent information.
- Reduced prevalence of harmful misinformation and its impact on public health.
- Enhanced global cooperation to ensure safer health practices and consumer protections.
- Strengthened trust in health systems through accountability and scientific integrity.

#10

Policy Proposal: Implementation of Advisory Boards Across All Necessary Government Agencies

Objective:

To enhance the efficiency, continuity, and expertise of government operations by integrating advisory boards comprised of former Senators and Representatives who meet eligibility criteria, thereby ensuring a steady flow of institutional knowledge and providing critical support to current legislators.

1. Purpose and Scope of Advisory Boards

- Establish **Advisory Boards** in all necessary government agencies to:
  - Provide institutional knowledge, historical context, and expert insights to current acting Senators and Representatives.
  - Support the resolution of complex policy issues by offering diverse perspectives and informed strategies.

2. Eligibility for Advisory Board Membership

- Former Senators and Representatives may serve on advisory boards if they meet the following criteria:
  - **Sound mind and health:** Verified through regular evaluations to ensure the ability to perform advisory duties effectively.
  - **Clear criminal record:** No ongoing investigations or convictions for criminal activities.
  - Demonstrated commitment to public service and policy expertise in their respective areas.

3. Advisory Role and Responsibilities

- Advisory board members will:
  - Serve under current acting Senators and Representatives to assist in addressing legislative challenges and decision-making processes.
  - Offer non-binding recommendations based on their experience and understanding of government operations.
  - Participate in strategy sessions, policy discussions, and crisis management initiatives as needed.

4. Acting as Interim Representatives

- Former Senators and Representatives on advisory boards may temporarily assume active roles under the following circumstances:
  - **Extended Absence of Acting Officials:**
    - If an acting Senator or Representative is unable to perform their duties for extended periods (e.g., beyond sick leave or

vacation), advisory board members may temporarily step in to ensure continuity of governance.
- This interim service requires formal approval from relevant government oversight committees and leadership bodies.
  ○ **Response to Crisis:**
    - In situations of national or regional crisis, eligible advisory board members may be appointed as acting Senators or Representatives to address immediate needs and implement resolutions until the regular officeholder returns or a replacement is formally elected or appointed.

5. Oversight and Accountability

- Advisory board members will operate under the **guidance and supervision of current government leadership** to maintain alignment with contemporary legislative priorities and public expectations.
- Clear documentation of advisory board activities and decisions will be maintained to ensure transparency and accountability.

6. Benefits of Implementation

- **Continuity of Leadership:**
  ○ Minimizes disruptions in legislative processes during unforeseen absences of acting officials.
- **Enhanced Policy-Making:**

- Leverages the knowledge and experience of seasoned legislators to navigate complex issues effectively.
- **Crisis Response:**
  - Ensures competent and immediate action during emergencies through the appointment of experienced advisory board members.

Expected Outcomes:

- Improved legislative performance through the integration of expert advisors.
- Reduced gaps in governance caused by absences or unexpected vacancies.
- Strengthened trust in government institutions by prioritizing informed decision-making and continuity of leadership.

#11

Policy Proposal: Liberation of Minds Within the American Population

Objective

To empower the American populace through education, transparency, and proactive measures against manipulative practices, ensuring mental liberation and the safeguarding of individual autonomy.

1. Establishment of a Research Task Force
Purpose:
Create a specialized task force to explore the phenomenon of mind control and its implications.

Responsibilities:

- Develop comprehensive legal definitions of mind control and related tactics.
- Investigate and document the psychological, social, and economic effects on victims of mind control.
- Identify populations most vulnerable to such tactics, including marginalized communities, isolated individuals, and those with limited access to education.

- Explore methods for deprogramming victims and supporting their reintegration into society.

2. Public Awareness Campaigns
Goals:

- Promote critical thinking and independent research within the general population.
- Educate the public on recognizing signs of propaganda, covert manipulation, and mind control tactics.

Execution:

- Partner with educational institutions, media outlets, and community organizations to disseminate accurate information.
- Enlist public figures, educators, and mental health professionals to advocate for the campaign.

3. Public Resources for Identifying Manipulation
Purpose:
Provide accessible tools to help individuals identify and counteract manipulation tactics.

Content Includes:

- Guidelines for recognizing cult-like behaviors in groups.
- Information on covert influences such as propaganda, gaslighting, and emotional manipulation.
- Insights into tactics used by narcissists, sociopaths, and psychopaths.

Distribution Channels:

- Online platforms, public libraries, and mental health clinics.
- Community workshops and seminars.

4. Confidential Whistleblower Reporting System

Implementation:
Establish secure and confidential channels for reporting suspected cult activities or manipulative practices.

Protections for Whistleblowers:

- Guarantee anonymity and protection against retaliation.
- Provide emotional and legal support, including access to counseling and advocacy services.

5. Immediate Criminal Investigations

Mandate:
Launch thorough investigations into any group implicated in:

- Sudden disappearances of individuals.
- Intimidation or harassment of whistleblowers.
- Suspected involvement in the death of individuals linked to whistleblowing activities.

Execution:
Ensure investigations are impartial, regardless of the group's societal, religious, or political status.

6. Transparency and Accountability of Government Actions

Declassification of Mind Control Experiments:

- Declassify historical government experiments involving mind control to build public trust.
- Provide explanations for any legal or security obstacles preventing full disclosure.

Oversight Committees:

- Create independent committees to review declassified information and update the public.
- Allow public input on addressing findings related to past government actions.

7. Expected Outcomes

- **Empowered Populace:** A critically thinking public resistant to manipulation.
- **Enhanced Whistleblower Protections:** Increased reporting of harmful practices and greater accountability.
- **Trust and Transparency:** Strengthened trust in the government through disclosure and oversight.

Amendment: Protection of Minors Against Sexual Indoctrination

Criminalization of Sexual Indoctrination

Definition:

Sexual indoctrination refers to coercing, pressuring, or manipulating individuals under 18—or below the age of consent in their jurisdiction—into exposure to sexual imagery, practices, or risky gender identification ideologies without their informed consent.

Penalties:

- **Imprisonment:** Up to 30 years.
- **Professional Disqualification:** Permanent disqualification from roles involving minors.
- **Classification as a Violent Sexual Predator:** Mandatory registration and community notification.

Child-Centered Approach:

- Ensure decisions about gender identity or same-gender attraction are initiated by the child, free from external pressure.
- Provide unbiased resources for minors exploring their identity, respecting their autonomy and dignity.

Amendment: Safeguarding LGBTQ+ Community Protections

Respect for Protected Status:

- Uphold the rights of LGBTQ+ individuals, ensuring this policy does not stigmatize or target LGBTQ+ identities or relationships.
- Provide affirming, age-appropriate education about gender and sexual orientation.

Guidance for Schools and Institutions:

- Adhere to age-appropriate guidelines in educational programs to foster understanding without coercion.
- Maintain transparency with parents while safeguarding minors' privacy when exploring personal identity.

Implementation and Enforcement
Oversight and Investigation:

- Establish specialized units within law enforcement to investigate sexual indoctrination and exploitation claims.
- Train investigators to differentiate between supportive education and coercive practices.

Mandatory Reporting:

- Require teachers, caregivers, and healthcare professionals to report suspected cases.
- Protect whistleblowers with confidentiality and legal safeguards.

Educational Reforms:

- Develop clear curricula to distinguish appropriate education from coercive practices.
- Conduct regular audits to ensure compliance.

Expected Outcomes

- **Protection of Minors:** Strengthened safeguards against exploitation.

- **Support for Autonomy:** Empowered minors to make informed decisions about their identity.
- **Balanced Protections:** Clear differentiation between exploitative practices and legitimate support for LGBTQ+ youth.
- **Accountability:** Strict consequences for violations, promoting a culture of accountability and respect.

This amendment maintains a child-focused approach, ensuring robust protections while respecting individual rights and the LGBTQ+ community.

#12

Policy Proposal: Enhanced Cultural Understanding of Other Nations, Planets, and Realms

Objective:

To create a foundation for cultural awareness, education, and interconnectivity among Earth's nations and prepare for potential interactions with non-human intelligences (NHIs), including extraterrestrial or interdimensional beings. This proposal emphasizes the importance of transparency, education, and collaboration to foster unity, promote peace, and enhance understanding on a planetary and interstellar scale.

1. Strengthening Diplomatic Relations Among Earth Nations

- **Building Cooperative Frameworks:**

    - Strengthen existing international organizations and treaties to facilitate open dialogue and mutual understanding.
    - Host regular cultural summits where nations can showcase their traditions, innovations, and perspectives while addressing shared challenges

such as climate change, health crises, and economic inequality.

- **Promoting Cultural Awareness Through Diplomacy:**

  ○ Task diplomats with the dual role of addressing political and economic matters and becoming cultural ambassadors.

  ○ Publish their findings, experiences, and insights as a part of a global repository of cultural knowledge. These reports would help break down stereotypes and reduce geopolitical biases, fostering a more interconnected global community.

2. Expanding Cultural Education Programs

- **Curriculum Development:**

  ○ Introduce robust cultural studies courses in schools that cover the history, traditions, and modern challenges of various nations.

  ○ Include modules addressing global issues, such as public health, technological disparities, and human rights concerns.

- **Funding and Accessibility:**

  ○ Provide federal grants to schools for implementing cultural exchange programs, including virtual reality experiences simulating life in other countries.

- Fund student travel opportunities to engage with other cultures firsthand, covering costs such as passports, visas, vaccinations, and transportation.

- **Safety Protocols:**

  - Create detailed safety plans for students traveling to areas with potential risks, ensuring proper vetting and parental consent for all travel.

- **Reflective Learning:**

  - Require students to document their experiences in travel journals, essays, or multimedia projects.
  - Compile these materials into an evolving cultural education library accessible to future participants and educators.

3. Establishing a Publishing Outlet for Cultural Works

- **Global Access and Promotion:**

  - Create a publishing platform for diplomats, students, and educators to share their cultural findings.
  - Collaborate with global institutions to promote these works and distribute them in various languages to maximize reach.

- **Supporting Authors:**

- Offer authors the choice to earn royalties or donate proceeds to further cultural education initiatives, ensuring their contributions are recognized.
- **Community Engagement:**

  - Organize events, such as book readings, discussions, and workshops, to showcase published works and foster dialogue about cultural understanding.

---

4. Engaging with Non-Human Intelligences (NHIs)

- **Establishing Diplomatic Protocols:**

  - Develop secure communication channels and protocols for engaging with extraterrestrial or interdimensional entities.
  - Prioritize peaceful interaction, mutual respect, and cooperation in these exchanges.
- **Transparency and Trust:**

  - Fully declassify government research and information on extraterrestrial phenomena, ensuring public access.
  - Address potential limitations or redactions by providing clear explanations of any withheld information.
- **Encouraging Knowledge Sharing:**

- Foster goodwill by promoting reciprocal exchanges of knowledge and technology with NHIs.
    - Create interdisciplinary research teams to study and adapt technologies or insights shared by NHIs for public benefit.
- **Integrating Extraterrestrial Perspectives into Education:**

    - Introduce verified accounts of alien abductions or communications into educational materials, encouraging critical analysis and open-mindedness.
    - Offer platforms for individuals who have experienced extraterrestrial encounters to share their stories, ensuring respect and validation of their experiences.
- **Expanding Travel Opportunities:**

    - Extend cultural education programs to include interstellar travel, contingent upon thorough safety evaluations and diplomatic agreements.
    - Ensure that participants are well-prepared for physical, psychological, and cultural challenges associated with such ventures.

---

5. Broader Impacts and Benefits

- **Global Unity:**

- Strengthened international cooperation will promote peace and shared progress, reducing geopolitical tensions.

- **Informed and Empowered Population:**

  - A well-rounded, culturally educated citizenry will be better equipped to address global challenges and embrace diversity.

- **Public Trust in Governance:**

  - Increased transparency, especially regarding extraterrestrial phenomena, will bolster public confidence in government actions and policies.

- **Foundation for Interstellar Engagement:**

  - Preparing for interactions with NHIs will position humanity as a thoughtful and collaborative species, capable of contributing meaningfully to interstellar communities.

Implementation Timeline and Phases

1. **Phase 1: Establish Foundational Programs (Year 1-2)**

   - Launch cultural summits and initial educational modules in schools.
   - Establish the global publishing platform for cultural works.

2. **Phase 2: Expand Public Engagement (Year 3-5)**

- ○ Begin funding and facilitating travel programs for students.
- ○ Initiate declassification of extraterrestrial phenomena and develop diplomatic protocols for NHI engagement.

3.   **Phase 3: Deepen Global and Interstellar Ties (Year 6-10)**

- ○ Expand interstellar travel opportunities.
- ○ Incorporate findings from NHIs into educational and technological development programs.

Conclusion

The *Enhanced Cultural Understanding of Other Nations, Planets, and Realms* policy envisions a future where humanity transcends boundaries—whether national or interstellar—by embracing diversity, fostering education, and building trust. This approach not only strengthens the bonds among Earth's nations but also prepares for humanity's potential role as a thoughtful and responsible member of a broader cosmic community.

DAKOTA'S NOMINATION INFORMATION

Bio: https://www.linkedin.com/in/dakota-frandsen-545b12176/

Resume or CV: https://www.linkedin.com/in/dakota-frandsen-545b12176/

Writing or Publications: www.baldandbonkers.net

Website: www.baldandbonkers.net

Video: https://www.youtube.com/@BaldandBonkers

Socials:

Agency or agencies for which nominator feels nominee is best suited:

- Central Intelligence Agency
- Department of Homeland Security
- Department of Justice
- U.s. Agency for Global Media
- Small Business Administration

Organization name(s) and position(s) for which nominator feels nominee is best suited:

Policies which the nominator knows the nominee supports or in which they have expertise:

Term Limits for Senators and Representatives, An Entrepreneurial Ecosystem, Therapy for First-Responders, and in Professional/School Settings, New frontiers for Victims of Abuse + Criminal Activity, Modern-Day Mind Control: The Information War, Covert Influences, PsyOps, + Cult Deprogramming; Public Support for Law Enforcement Officers; Rehabilitation Accessiblity for Addicts; Criminalization of Tobacco Products

Nominator's thoughts on what would make this nominee a valuable member of a future Trump Unity Government
1) Is Competent ...
2) Is Honest...
3) Is Respectful ...
4) Has Integrity ...
5) Has Courage ...
6) Has a Proven Record...
Dakota Frandsen, founder of Bald and Bonkers Network LLC, possesses the character and competence to serve the people of the United States with honor, honesty, respect, integrity, courage, and proven success. Through his network, Dakota offers resources, inspiration, and encouragement to prospective entrepreneurs in any pursuit, no matter how unorthodox or difficult. His candor in describing paranormal experiences also provided a comfortable, empathetic

environment for those who experienced traumatic situations and adversity, further affording them the opportunity to tell their stories of survival and re-siliency. His commitment to helping others have available-to-all, accurate information with empathy is a reflection of his skill and passion as an advocate and a leader.

1) Competency

Competencies of practice, time and again, Dakota has shown through his research-based approach to the strategic development of Bald and Bonkers Network LLC. He has also shown much foresight with respect to marketplace demands, resource handling, and the subtlety involved in the growth of a business when establishing and developing this platform. In so do-ing, Dakota reveals an adaptable and forward-think-ing approach by investing in the development of tailored resources for budding entrepreneurs-partic-ularly those engaged in some rather unconventional industries and pursuits. It also testifies to his ability and commitment in a brutal industry where only the most resilient and capable survive.

2) Honesty

Dakota's sincerity is not just confined to his way of conducting business but further builds into his per-sonal experiences with the paranormal. He openly shares his encounters and experiences so that others feel comfortable enough to share their stories-mostly trauma, mental health struggles, or survival against all odds. Among his biggest strengths is transparency: Dakota brings empathy and realism to both his discussions on the supernatural and business-oriented topics, which helps him foster trust among his audience. His commitment to truth fosters a community based on an emerging tapestry of shared experiences, where people can come together and find healing in supportive company.

3) Respect

Dakota respects individuality and diversity, as reflected in his work with Bald and Bonkers Network LLC and his support of people from all walks of life. His platform is inclusive of all walks of life, from the most misunderstood to those that have been marginalized because of their experiences or interests. Dakota respected the private journey of every soul, from trauma victims to those who fought with poor mental and physical health. He gives them an outlet, building a platform of mutual respect and trust where people can open up and begin to heal through the process of storytelling.

4) Integrity

Integrity is simply what it is-the cornerstone of Dakota's personal life and professional practices. His sense of morals in ethics and commitment to personal morality is what dictates interaction and choice. Dakota doesn't compromise on standing for what is right: from advocating ethical businesses to providing a platform where people can share supernatural or personal struggles. He infuses the same integrity into the mission of his company-to provide quality resources and build resilience-by ensuring that every act contributes toward the greater good rather than profit. The integrity of Dakota is unshaken, which makes him one of the few trusted leaders who can genuinely assure of infusing a positive change.

5) Courage

Dakota is brave to speak to people who have experiences and ideas usually considered unconventional or taboo. He is himself open and vocal with the supernatural things he has gone through, and this open way brings out others to tell their stories; it takes a rare bravery. Dakota's willingness to go through "strange and stressful" experiences, such as survival stories about people in trauma, mental health struggles, and physical pain, only shows fearlessness regarding creating a safe and inclusive space. It is his courage to tell personal stories and encourage others to do so that gives hope and solidarity to many.

6) Track Record

As an accomplished entrepreneur, mentor, and advocate, Dakota pulls effectiveness through leadership. Providing resources through Bald and Bonkers Network LLC, rapidly becoming a trusted platform where entrepreneurs can find the guidance they need to fulfill their goals, no matter how out of the box.

This extends beyond business. His blunt conversations about the supernatural and trauma have inspired countless individuals who no longer feel ashamed to tell their stories and seek help. Dakota's history of success proves he can accomplish much to bring about long-term, positive change, and with his care for others, he has the potential to serve the American people with honor.

Conclusion

Dakota Frandsen is a compassionate, courageous, and capable leader. He has shown, through his truthful sharing of the supernatural encounters, how much he cares for the creation of a safe space for trauma survivors. It is through competence, honesty, respect, integrity, courage, and proven records of success that Dakota leads-qualities that further strengthen his position as a leader and advocate for change. Through Bald and Bonkers Network LLC, Dakota provides hands-on tools for upcoming entrepreneurs, but also a platform where one finds hope through others, shares experiences, and builds resilience. In his commitment to people's empowerment, added to his high moral standing and commitment to inclusivity, he is an exemplary service to the people of the United States.

Dakota Frandsen is a visionary entrepreneur, writer, and advocate for cultural understanding and personal growth. As the CEO and founder of Bald and Bonkers Network LLC, Dakota has dedicated his life to creating platforms that empower individuals to share their stories and embrace their true selves. His work spans across various fields, including multimedia production, educational programs, and public outreach, with a particular focus on the supernatural, mental health, and global connectivity.

Having spent years as a paranormal expert, known as the "Specialist of the Strange," Dakota has built a reputation for his deep curiosity about the unknown and his ability to connect diverse audiences. His passion for fostering inclusivity, personal development, and the pursuit of truth has led him to develop projects such as Bald and Bonkers Network Academy, a platform designed to help entrepreneurs and creatives build their brands.

In addition to his business endeavors, Dakota is also the author of several works that reflect his interest in mental health, self-discovery, and the exploration of supernatural phenomena. His writing blends personal reflection with a keen sense of mystery and introspection, capturing both the complexity of human emotions and the vast potential for growth and healing.

Through his work, Dakota strives to build a community where everyone is empowered to understand themselves and the world around them—whether that world be earthly or beyond.

www.ingramcontent.com/pod-product-compliance
Lightning Source LLC
Chambersburg PA
CBHW010031180726
47992CB00025B/3396